Wonders of the World
of the Albatross

Wonders of the World of the Albatross

Harvey I. Fisher and Mildred L. Fisher

ILLUSTRATED WITH PHOTOGRAPHS BY HARVEY I. FISHER

Dodd, Mead & Company · New York

To the eager children of the world. May their delightful curiosity about nature never cease.

Frontispiece: Laysan Albatrosses on Midway Atoll.

Acknowledgments

For nearly a score of years our scientific studies of the Laysan Albatross have benefitted from the financial support and good will of many organizations. Dozens of individual persons have also helped in dozens of ways.

We cannot here express our appreciation to all who have so freely given of their money and time. The investigations which provided the background for this book would have been impossible without the continuous and diverse support of Southern Illinois University, Carbondale. The Office of Naval Research, the American Philosophical Society, and the National Geographic Society provided funds. Many graduate students gave generously of their own time on Midway Atoll.

The United States naval commands on the island and the people of Midway were understanding and cooperative.

Miss Dorothy Bryan, our editor, labored long and hard to enable us to reach still another audience—the young people—with the story of the Laysan Albatross.

To all these, and to the unnamed as well, we say, "Thank you very much."

Harvey I. Fisher and Mildred L. Fisher

Contents

Albatrosses are fearless but gentle.

1. What Is an Albatross?

Albatrosses are big and gentle birds. Some kinds weigh only six pounds, others as much as twenty pounds. Males and females look alike, but the males are slightly heavier and taller. The distance between the wing tips of the smallest ones is six feet, while on the largest it may be as much as eleven feet. The bigger albatrosses are by far the largest oceanic birds.

The albatrosses are the birds most often observed by people traveling on ships on the high seas, for they spend most of their lives on or over the ocean waters and come to land only to breed. They migrate for thousands of miles. Their long, narrow, pointed wings, which are powered by massive breast muscles, can use oceanic currents to good advantage. Also, the three front toes, which are strong and webbed, make excellent paddles for swimming. Wide, hard, white feathers cover the body and protect a thick underlayer of air-filled downy feathers. The down, which

Tubular nostrils characterize albatrosses and their relatives.

insulates against the cold air and water, also buoys up the weight of the albatross. The bird floats high and dry and is nearly unsinkable. Albatrosses do not dive for food. They catch squid (marine mollusks without shells) and small fishes near the water's surface.

Albatrosses belong to a group of birds called "procellariiformes"—a formidable name for friendly and often amusing creatures. The word means "tube-nosed," and was selected by scientists because the nostrils of the albatross end in a pair of small tubes high on the bill. The bill itself is stout and hooked into a pointed tip. It is covered with shiny, horny plates, and the long edges are razor-keen.

There are more than fifty varieties of shearwaters and two dozen species of petrels, the small relatives of albatrosses which are much like them in appearance and habits. Albatrosses and these close kin number more than ninety kinds of birds. All of them belong to the Order Procellariiformes.

These are ancient birds. Fossils of ten species have been found in rocks. Some of them lived fifty million years ago. Much of the early information about albatrosses came from observations by uneducated and often superstitious men on whaling ships. Shipboard stories about these birds passed from man to man, and from generation to generation of men. The sailor folklore was cleverly written into tales of the sea and became legends. In the minds of many readers and listeners, such fanciful stories as that of *The Rime of the Ancient Mariner* became fact. Since 1950, however, scientists have learned a great deal about the dozen kinds of albatrosses that still roam the seas.

Their nests are built on the ground. Incubation occupies from nine to twelve weeks, and the chick is fed by the two parents for from twenty-four to fifty-two weeks, varying with the kind of albatross. Their periods of incubation and chick care are the longest known.

As scientists—trained and enthused ornithologists—we have learned much by banding young albatrosses on Midway Atoll in the North Pacific Ocean. The residents of Midway call the albatrosses "gooney birds." No one is certain how this name arose, but it may refer to the birds' comical antics on land.

During June of several summers we walked among the young birds, gently catching each one. We encircled one leg with a

Laysan Albatross and chick.

Mildred Fisher, one of the authors of this book, finds a newly arrived albatross in the brush of a Pacific atoll.

narrow, numbered band and joined the metal ends carefully so there were no sharp edges to injure the nestlings. Perhaps their indignation at being grabbed, lifted, and upended was so great they forgot about the tiny weight of the band, for we never saw a bird so much as look or peck at its new jewelry.

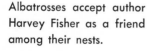

Albatrosses accept author Harvey Fisher as a friend among their nests.

A band on an albatross leg can tell the scientist many things.

By catching these banded albatrosses many different times in later years, on land and at sea, we found out how long they lived, when they first visited their home island, when they chose their mates, when they first nested, whether they came back to the same place each season, where they spent their time on the ocean, how long a pair stayed together to breed, and a great many other characteristic and interesting things about their habits.

Most albatrosses live in the cold, subantarctic seas of the Southern Hemisphere. The Wandering Albatross and the Royal Albatross are the largest of the southern albatrosses. Other kinds have such unusual names as Black-browed and Yellow-nosed and Sooty. The Waved Albatross lives on the Galapagos Islands near the equator. Only three kinds live north of the equator. These are the Black-footed Albatross, the Short-tailed Albatross, and the Laysan Albatross.

This book is about the world of the Laysan Albatross, *Diomedea immutabilis*. Although it is one of the smaller species, its life story is fairly typical of that of most albatrosses.

2. Albatross Islands

Laysan Albatrosses live in the North Pacific Ocean—an area twice as large as the North Atlantic Ocean. The millions of square miles of the North Pacific are bounded on the north by the Aleutian Islands. This beadlike string of tiny islands, extending westward from Alaska, forms a kind of fence. The islands of Japan mark the western edge, while the shores of the North American continent are the eastern limits of their domain. To the south the birds seek their breeding grounds on islands of the Hawaiian chain, but south of Hawaii unsuitably warm, tropical waters and a scarcity of food combine to keep the Laysan Albatrosses to the north.

In this vast North Pacific range the water temperatures are between 40 and 70 degrees Fahrenheit. The area provides a bountiful supply of their favorite food—squid—and Laysans occur all over this region, but, naturally, they are most numerous where temperatures and food are best.

Thousands of Laysans nest side by side on Midway.

Since the food supply changes with the seasons, and since the Laysan Albatrosses must go to land to breed, the birds move seasonally—migrating to islands where they mate, produce a single egg, and incubate their chick.

Not all islands are satisfactory for breeding. Some, near the ocean's shores, are the tops of mountains whose bottoms rest on the continental shelf. Laysans do not use these islands which are generally large, high, forested, and much used by people.

They nest on islands like Kure, Midway, Pearl and Hermes, Lisianski, French Frigate, and Laysan of the Hawaiian chain. All of these preferred islands are small, flat, have few or no human residents, and are in the middle of the ocean. Ornithologists first discovered our albatross on Laysan Island in the 1890s, and that is how the species received its name of Laysan Albatross.

These islands were formed by ancient volcanoes that erupted

15

from the floor of the sea. Time after time, the fiery volcanoes spewed out and, each time, their lava cinder cones became higher. Some eventually extended a thousand or more feet above the sea's surface. Then, in later years, the ocean rose hundreds of feet and covered some of these projecting volcanoes. Others were left with only their tips above water. Tiny coral animals fastened their microscopic, rocklike skeletons atop the submerged and now dead volcanoes or around their protruding edges, where the seawaves lapped at the lava. As the ocean continued to rise, coral grew upward on coral, always toward the light. Some layers, composed of billions of these minute skeletons, became seven hundred feet thick. In time, even the tops of the tallest of these lava cones were covered with coral, and all that showed above the water was a circle of coral reef surrounding a shallow, coral-bottomed lagoon. Some of these lagoons in albatross land are twenty miles across, but that of Midway Atoll, a favored breeding place of the Laysan Albatross, is only five.

Turbulent seas continued to push coral sand and coral rock onto the reef, which formed small islands. Later storms scattered some of the accumulated sand back into the sea. The islands of coral that withstood the waves were flat and perched insecurely on the reef, only a few feet above the sea. Storms, at times, washed over the lowest ones.

This process of island formation continues today. Live coral grows on top of the remains of dead coral, and storms add to and subtract other materials from the reef. The outlines of the little, pancakelike islands change constantly. The waves and passing currents still bring plant seeds from distant lands and cast them ashore, to lodge between pebbles of sand. Only a few kinds of seeds can survive and grow in the infertile, salty soil. Their roots hold the sand and stony rubble together, more sand washes in,

16

and the island becomes permanent. The soil can support only scrubby growths. Wide expanses of sand and pieces of coral cover most of the islands.

These coral atolls in the western Hawaiian Islands are the chosen albatross islands. Here, the female Laysan scratches out a nest in the porous gravel, among the low bushes which shelter the nest from blowing sand and cold winds. But bushes are scant protection against the boiling ocean waves which sometimes surge and swirl in, to wash away eggs and nests.

On the other hand, no large animals that would disturb albatrosses ever came to these lonely atolls. The pioneer albatrosses never learned fear. None of these birds had ever seen a person on land until about 150 years ago, when men in ships explored the surrounding seas and hunted whales. Then, later, people came to live on these islands. With the people came pets—dogs and canaries, and sometimes rabbits. An unnoticed passenger was the house rat, which eats albatross eggs and an occasional, unguarded chick.

These tiny, sandspit islands of the North Pacific Ocean became important to men, as well as to birds. Albatrosses need ground for their nests. Men need it, also, to serve as stepping-stones from continent to continent—landing fields, refueling stations, military outposts, and homes for people.

Midway Atoll, one of these outposts, has two islands on its sixteen-mile reef. Sand Island, the larger one, is a mile and a half long and three-quarters of a mile wide. Eastern Island is three-quarters by one-fourth mile in size. About one-third of the world's Laysan Albatrosses breed on these two islands' sixteen hundred acres.

Midway is sometimes hot in the daytime of summer and cold on winter nights. The seasons here are during the same months as those in continental United States. Although 50 degrees is the

17

Laysan nests dot the shady lawns on Midway Atoll.

lowest usual temperature, it is a chilly 50 for man and bird when the moist, dank winds steal away the body's warmth. It is neither a tropical paradise nor a land of snow and ice. The seas temper the land, however, warming Midway in winter and cooling it in summer. The winters are no more than three months long, marked mostly by day after day of rain. Each storm is short, though. The clouds loose their moisture and move on. Breezes or winds are almost constant. There is no smog or fog, the air is sparkling clean, and the colors are intense. The red flowers of hibiscus and geranium, and the greens of the ironwood trees, all planted by man, contrast sharply with the white-yellows of the coral and sand.

The albatrosses nested undisturbed on Midway until 1903, when the Commercial Cable Company established a station on

18

Sand Island, to relay messages between North America and the Orient. It was manned by half a dozen people. They transported beach grass from San Francisco and ironwood trees from Australia, to help hold the sand in place. A small garden, grown in soil hauled in on ships, and a milk cow furnished part of the food, for supply ships arrived several months apart—when they arrived at all. Later, Pan American Airways used Midway as a refueling stop for their seaplanes which pioneered the air lanes across the Pacific.

Today, the birds share Midway with the United States Navy, and there is rivalry between the people and the birds for the small amount of land. The working and living quarters of the Navy men and their families take up much space. There are homes, stores, clubs, tennis courts, a theater, and even a golf course for the two thousand or so human residents. Paved roads, airstrips, and trees are on land where the albatrosses used to nest. Like it or not, many of the birds must now build their nests in the middle of man's island civilization. Midway is the only

Chick and child confront each other under the watchful eye of the mother of one of them.

Laysan Albatrosses compete with a variety of human activities for breeding space on Midway.

place in the world where albatrosses nest on a military base.

They nest on lawns near houses and stores and beside the busy roadways. They even land and stroll on the blacktopped streets. Pedestrians, bicycles, and trucks can only try to dodge the running, walking, flying birds. A truck stops to let a bird pass safely. Then truck and bird remain motionless in the middle of the road, confronting one another silently. Perhaps the driver

The earlier settlers, the albatrosses, feel that the island belongs to them.

honks and the bird nonchalantly saunters off, or, more fre-
quently, the driver disgustedly climbs down to shoo the albatross out of the way.

Most of the human residents of Midway enjoy watching the
albatrosses. Children and even crawling babies play with them.
But, once in a while, someone objects to the albatrosses setting
up housekeeping on his lawn and destroys the birds' nests and
eggs. And when albatrosses and airplanes try to use the same
landing strips at the same time, the birds are sometimes killed
and the planes damaged.

Laysan Albatrosses are very close neighbors to each other on
land, although they are seldom together when at sea. Nearly
two hundred thousand albatrosses breed on Midway, and perhaps a million non-breeding albatrosses visit Midway in late winter and spring. Inevitably, the place becomes noisy and crowded.

But by August, the bird colony on Midway is quiet and bare.
The Laysan Albatrosses of all ages have departed for their
oceanic home in the northwest part of the Pacific Ocean. No
albatrosses of any age can be found there until November, when
their wondrous world on land begins for the next generation.

Laysan Albatrosses share the beaches of Midway Island with United States Navy
men, their families, and their pets.

3. Incubating the Egg

It was a beautiful autumn day in the week before Thanksgiving. The warm sun shone through the clear air over Midway, and the trade winds came softly from the southeast, stirring into motion only the smallest green tips of the tallest ironwood trees. Thousands of Laysan Albatrosses had returned, and so had we, ornithologists studying this albatross. The lawns and fields were speckled with the birds' white and dappled black bodies. Males stood or rested on their bellies. Here and there, a female scurried to her mate.

All through the bird colony, and the human colony, there was a feeling of hushed anticipation. The male albatrosses expected their mates. The people, most of whom had never witnessed this seasonal invasion by a flood of winged residents, looked forward to an unusual experience. Neither the albatrosses nor the humans were disappointed.

A male, going to his territory, dodges the slashing attack of a male already on his own bit of land.

Each day, more and more of the big birds silently glided in between the tree trunks and over the bushes. Each day, the colony became noisier and more crowded and, as when people jam together, trouble brewed. Male albatrosses tolerated not even accidental trespassing by birds trying to find a safe path through the gathering. Resident males snapped their bills and screamed dire threats of future beatings, should the trespassers ever again chance to step on private property.

A male albatross must have a bit of land he owns, his territory. This provides him with the privacy he needs for courting the females and for his chosen female's nest in future years. Once he gains this three- to four-foot circular area, it is his lifelong possession. The first thing the young male must do, therefore, to prepare for reproducing his kind, is to search out a suitable, unclaimed territory on the island where he was hatched. He visits

23

there several times in each of his third, fourth, and fifth years, to find a desirable spot and to make it his, as we describe in Chapter 7.

It was well that the eight-year-old male of the pair whose story we are telling, landed at the sparsely occupied edge of the colony, for he was not mobbed immediately. Only two alert and distrustful males challenged him as he moved toward his own vacant territory. One of his neighbors had expanded a little too far into that territory, but a few threatening rushes, punctuated by the victory screams of the eight-year-old, drove the intruder back.

Our male's mate arrived a few days earlier than usual, bumping and skidding into a landing not too far away, but unfortunately, too near some other males. They were paired with still absent females, but they rushed over to her. Before she regained her balance or settled her wings into place, they tried to mate with her. As they fought and shrieked and tumbled on one another, she ducked out from under the pile-up and ran to her own mate. Although she was frightened and still badly ruffled up, she was safe here, because no other male dared enter her mate's territory.

The two touched bills gently and quickly, *eh, eh*ed a few times, and lowered themselves to the ground. In less than an hour, they began to preen one another and to prepare for mating. After mating, they winged southwest into the wind that was white-capping the small waves in Midway's lagoon, beginning their oceanic honeymoon. This interlude at sea always precedes the laying of the egg and the long and difficult time of incubation.

The female returned alone, six days after she had left on the honeymoon. Quickly, she scraped out a nest hollow in the moist sand, among the dry stems of last summer's weeds. She was troubled, though. A nearby female, also ready to lay her egg, was too close. The two of them rested on their breasts in their intended nests and squabbled and muttered at each other. They grabbed bills and tugged. When the bill battles became too fierce, one or both backed away an inch or so. After several such fracases and retreats, they could no longer touch each other.

In this way, the females space their nests, out of reach of their neighbors. As long as they cannot touch, neither they nor their males need fight during the endless days on the egg. The struggles might break the eggs, so it is best to resolve these conflicts before there are any eggs. These relations with neighboring females are the females' business, just as territorial relations are settled male-to-male. Seldom is there any kind of fight between a male and a female albatross.

The female's egg came four hours after her return. Her mate returned at noon the next day, and she stood up and let the egg slide out of her pouch. Males as well as females have a pouch. It is formed by down feathers dropping from a spot near the front of the belly. This leaves a baseball-sized cavity between the bare skin and the stiff outer feathers. Hot blood coursing through the skin heats the egg for its development. The stiff feathers below the egg protect it from the wet, cold sand.

Both albatrosses bent over and peered at this wondrous bit of life-to-be. The male *eh eh*ed and preened his mate. She settled back on the egg, reluctant to give up her incubation duties. He preened her again. With one foot in the nest and the other pushing from the side, he tried to shove her off. After several unsuccessful attempts, he got up and stalked around her twice. He bowed, preened her, and flicked some of his breast feathers. When she showed the egg again, he stepped right into the nest and pushed her out roughly.

The instinctive urge to keep the egg warm is a "spell" that forces both male and female birds to stay on the egg. The "spell" must be broken by the actions and sounds made by the returning mate. The preening, *eh eh*ing, bowing, circling, and pushing are the acts of the exchange ceremony that release the incubating bird from these powerful instincts and permit its mate to take charge of the egg.

Now that the exchange was actually made, the mother lost interest in egg and mate. She shook and, without a single backward glance, spread her wings into the strong wind and rose to sail and bank her way toward the sea. For a time, she was free of family cares—but not entirely, for now she must feed and get ready for her next turn at incubating.

The male began to finish the nest, which was one of his duties while he incubated this first time. He reached out, stuck the sharp tip of his bill into the ground, and dragged a pinch of sand and dirt toward himself. He grabbed a billful of ironwood needles and threw them against his side. Next came some leaves, laid

The female of our pair scratches out her nest saucer, unmolested by a male on an adjacent territory.

She bill-battles with a female who came too near, while a neutral spectator looks on calmly.

at his other side. As his bill picked and dragged, he rotated, taking material from a circle around the nest. The weight of his body tamped and shaped the inside of the bowl formed by the loose sand. By keeping his egg pouch and the egg within it on the tops of his toes as he wriggled about, he prevented the egg from being buried by the newly added materials that rolled inside the bowl.

The male used the sides of his bill to press and trowel down the outer slopes of the nest. This firming and smoothing made a tighter surface that rain and wind could not so easily wash or blow away. During the twenty-four days of his first time on the egg, he repaired the nest whenever the sand grains were wet enough to stick together. And this was often, for Midway in winter is a moist land. Each day, he turned the egg so all sides of it were properly warmed. Not once did he leave the nest.

Toward the end of his stay, he was hungry and thirsty. Going without food or water in the blustery winter weather had cost him a fourth of his body weight. The earlier stored fat was used up. Salt water no longer dripped from his bill, and he would soon have to go to sea to drink, as we explain in Chapter 6. His leg and wing muscles were cramped from setting so long, although he had stood and stretched whenever wind and temperature permitted. The machinery inside his body had slowed down, and he sat in a trance.

It was no wonder he was excited when his female came back. She was sleek and fat and rested. She now weighed more than the haggard male who rose to greet her and to show the egg. But, surprisingly, he at first didn't want to leave. Finally, he flew off.

Fifteen hundred miles away, and for twenty days, he slept as he floated, drank salt water, and ate numberless squid in the storm-tossed seas. One tempest bothered him a great deal, and it moved southeast to lash Midway with high winds and torrents of water. His female on the nest turned to face the roaring blasts and squatted low. She pulled an inner, somewhat transparent "third eyelid" across each eye. It provided some protection from the storm and still permitted some vision. Her feathers flattened to form a waterproof cover. But the flowing, stinging sand and pelting rain finally forced her to shut her eyes completely, by closing her upper and lower eyelids. She sat tight and kept the egg warm as the drops of water bounced off her oiled feathers. The rain fell so fast that not even the porous sand around the nest could soak it up. The water became four inches deep outside the nest, but the egg inside the bowl was an inch above water, and still dry. Luckily, the storm moved on within twenty-four hours, and the flooding waters seeped off.

Like her mate, she lost weight as her twenty days passed. She, too, incubated in a trancelike daze.

Her male was in excellent condition when he returned to Mid-

The male, who has just relieved his mate from incubation duties, joins her in "talking to the egg."

way. The pair exchanged places, and he immediately built up the storm-damaged nest, which the female had not fully repaired. The alternation of nest duty and recuperation at sea continued with the period shortening appreciably each time, until the egg had incubated for a total of sixty-five days.

In the last of these days, late in January and just before it broke from the prisonlike egg, the chick learned to recognize the voices of its mother and father. The chick had to respond to either one of them the very first day it was out of the shell, if it was to receive food. So, in the three or four days just before hatching, the adult on duty bent over and *eh eh*ed, with its bill almost touching the egg. We call it "talking to the egg," but the parents were really signaling to the chick inside, recording their voices forever in the brain of the youngster.

Before the eggs hatched this year, we wanted to find out the results of an experiment we had started the previous August. We hoped to find out how an albatross finds its own little space among all the others, although how they found their island initially was still a mystery. With surveying instruments and tape measures, we charted the exact locations of hundreds of nests. The birds using each nest, and the nests themselves were numbered. Next we removed every landscape feature we thought the birds might use to get back to their homes. We cut down all the trees and brush and hauled them away. We pulled up the weeds, and even the nest-marking stakes. With rake and hoe, we flattened hillocks and filled in hollows, until that part of the colony was as featureless as a newly seeded lawn. We knew from earlier observations that our changes in the colony would not prevent the return of the birds or keep them from breeding. It seemed to us, however, that they might not come back to the same exact spot.

We compared their nest locations this season with the numbers on our charts, for each pair of birds. No pair was nesting more than four feet from the nest place of the previous year! The birds had found their territories, even after we had removed the landmarks—but we still did not know how they did it. Our astonishment and pleasure at the birds' abilities went on all season, as each pair returned on schedule to its completely altered home-site.

4. Growing Up

The chick was ready to hatch. Inside the egg, it bent forward, into a half-moon. Suddenly, it straightened out, and there was a faint click as the stiff egg tooth on the tip of the chick's bill hit the inside of the hard shell. Time after time, the chick bent, straightened, and thrust the tooth against the shell. Each time a series of clicks sounded, like the slow ticking of a grandfather's clock, the mother stood to watch and to talk to the egg. Hours later, the chick had made a large enough hole in the shell to take its first breath of Midway's air. This tiny break in the shell and a piece pushed outward by the egg tooth is the first sign of hatching. It is called pipping.

During the following night, a second pip appeared, a quarter of an inch from the first. The chick was punching a scattered ring of holes around the large, blunt end of the egg. On the second day, the chick's stubby, gray bill, with its whitish egg

The baby albatross punches a hole through the shell and takes its first breath of Midway's clean air.

tooth, showed through one hole. The bill moved with each breath the chick took. By the third afternoon, there were four holes, and a faint, jagged crack connected two of them. The chick kicked away the blunt end of the shell near noon of the fourth day and rolled out. The wet and tired half-pound of new albatross struggled to stand, but couldn't. Its head was too heavy to hold up. The watching mother *eh eh*ed and then, because the wind was cold, stood over the chick. Her strong, webbed toes crushed the fragments of discarded shell. Carefully, she eased the rear end of the weak chick into her egg pouch, which now would serve as a chick pouch. The chick's rear end had to go in first so it could breathe at the open end of the pouch.

Late that same afternoon, the mother raised up to free the chick from its cozy feathered sack. She coaxed it to turn and face forward. Touching its bill with hers, she *eh eh*ed, to tell it that this was its mother's voice, urging it to take some food. She nibbled at the chick's bill. Still unable to stand or keep its head up, it turned its bill to the left, and the female touched it. The

32

baby opened its bill, and the mother dropped in a teaspoonful of thin brown oil. The smelly, rich mixture came from glands in the mother's stomach and from the fatty juices of digested squid. The father also produced this oily food, but he was miles away now and would not return for four more days. Until then, the youngster would depend upon its mother to regurgitate oil every few hours. But now, she tucked the baby back into her pouch.

A couple of hours later, she released the now dry and stronger baby. Its wings were only short stubs that didn't even show, and its feet were hidden below its body. As it turned in a half circle and raised its bill, it looked like a fluffy ball dipped in silvery cake icing. The mother gave it a little oil, then brooded it until the next morning.

Even before the sun's yellow halo broke over the horizon, the youngster was wiggling about, hungry again. This time, it raised up on trembling legs and opened its bill right away. Six times the baby swallowed oil before it was satisfied and went to sleep. The early sun was warm and the day's winds had not yet come, so the mother remained standing over her sleeping chick.

When the father arrived with food for the chick he had never seen, the pair gazed at their youngster. Then the mother flew off. The male touched the tip of his bill to the downy feathers, and the chick roused up to beg. The baby was always hungry. The male moved closer and fed it oil and tiny bits of squid each time the chick raised its bill. At night, the father brooded it. In the daytime, he sat at the edge of the nest, guarding.

There isn't really much to guard against on Midway, but guarding is an ancient tradition, brought north by albatross ancestors who came from the Antarctic, where predatory birds do snatch unprotected chicks right out of the nest. So the North Pacific albatrosses continue to guard—against nothing.

The baby begs for food by touching its father's bill.

When the female returned a couple of days later, the young-ster stood up and touched her bill. It pointed its bill straight up and *peeped* feebly, then touched her bill again. The baby had learned to beg properly and to put his open bill crosswise, be-tween the top and bottom parts of the bill of whichever parent was feeding it.

After this feeding, the female sat near the nest and guarded her chick for the last time. Those two weeks of being guarded by the parents were past. From now until the day it left the colony, the chick would stay alone and be visited and fed only once each day by one of the parents, which alternated in this duty.

By coming in only every other day, each parent had more time to fly farther in the search for squid—and we learned from a little experiment that these birds sometimes travel hundreds of miles on a single feeding trip.

34

One April day, we sprayed the heads of some breeding birds with bright paint, and the Commanding Officer at Midway asked all ships to report any painted albatrosses they saw. One ship, more than a thousand miles away, observed seven Laysans with topknots of our red paint. Since we knew each bird was feeding a chick every other day, we also knew these birds must have flown at least this distance, back and forth, in no more than a day or so.

A growing young albatross demands more and more food until, near the end of its nest life, it is fed a pound or more of squid each day. A three-pound baby with a pound of food inside resembles a bursting, pear-shaped sack. Both parents are needed to supply sufficient food. One parent alone simply can't bring in enough squid, so, if one parent dies, the chick starves. Happily, this doesn't occur very often.

While the parents are away, the chick has little to do except

A month-old chick is filled to bursting by a one-pound meal of squid and oil.

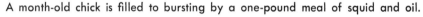

sleep and grow. For the first month, the nest is its protective haven and it does not venture far away. The rims of the old nest bowl are partly worn down and scattered by now. As leaves and sand are blown into the nest, the chick regularly scratches them out.

By doing this, the young bird maintains a foxhole for a shelter. Strong, wintry blasts occasionally go on for days and may actually blow away the entire fragile, sandy nest, which leaves the chick exposed. All it can do then is face the wind to keep its feathers smooth. Ruffled feathers let the rain in and the body heat out. Then the chick becomes chilled. Facing in the best direction, it pulls its head and neck back between its shoulders, closes its eyes, and sits out the storm. In unprotected places, the whistling gusts pile sand around the squatting chick—and occasionally cover it completely.

Being in a hole is of no help at all, though, when several inches of rain fall in a half day. The downy feathers, unlike the hard feathers of adults, do not form a very waterproof covering. The young albatross is drenched to the skin, chilled, and thoroughly miserable.

Some people think that having baby albatrosses hatch in the middle of winter is all wrong. This is not true. Most chicks do survive these difficult times, with help from their parents. Since the young birds need five or six months to grow up enough to take care of themselves, it is best for them to hatch just that long before the winter storms die off and the seas calm. As it is, then, the young and inexperienced birds can go to sea at the best possible time, to find squid and to make their way to the albatross "nursery."

Within six weeks of hatching, the chick walks short distances. However, life continues to be pretty monotonous. The highlight of each day, of course, is the return of a parent with food. Parent

The downy feathers of the growing chick are tipped with a silvery frosting.

and chick recognize each other instantly, and if the chick has moved away, it runs back to its father's territory immediately. It must, for that is the only place where either parent will feed it.

We proved this one year. A female laid her egg between the ruts of a little-used road. She had to duck each time the axles of a truck passed over her. We shoved a big piece of flat tin through the soft sand, six inches below her nest. Each day, we pulled the tin and nest a few more inches toward the side of the road. The parents incubated the egg successfully by the roadside, and fed the chick there for several weeks after it hatched. But as soon as the chick could walk easily, the parents made it come to the middle of the road, to the original nest place, before they would feed it. They had adjusted temporarily to our well-intentioned interference because of love for the egg and chick, but, as soon as possible, they went back to the traditional habits of their kind.

The big change at this walking stage is that the food is almost entirely squid, eight to ten inches long and a dozen to a meal! But after such a stuffing, a rest, and a sleep on the old nest, monotony sets in again. A few chicks try to preen their scraggly, tangled fuzz. They soon give up. Others play with leaves on overhanging bushes, and some just waddle and visit from neighbor to neighbor. Still others crawl right over to another bored chick and bite it. Perhaps the childish fight breaks up the day after day, lonely boredom. Neither youngster gets hurt, and the squabble passes the time. Any pile of leaves or sandy rise is soon a favorite place for chicks to sit and watch the world go by. They fight for the privilege of staying on such choice lookouts.

On hot summer days, the youngsters seek cooler places, of any kind—the sun-spotted shade of a thin weed, the shifting, rippling shadows cast by swaying branches of trees, or the solid shelter of tree trunks and parked trucks. The heavy down covering the body is much too warm now. Even out of the direct sun's rays, the birds pant, with bills open, dog fashion. To help cool themselves, they sit on their heels and raise their webbed feet off the hot ground. These webbed feet work like the radiators of cars. The breezes flow over and under the webs and cool the hot blood which runs between the thin layers of skin.

By June, when the albatrosses are about four months old, the dark feathers of the wings and tail are fully grown. Their bellies are white with new feathers. The matted down is gone, except on the neck and a topknot on the head. The youngsters exercise their wing muscles, which is the first step in preparing to leave the colony. At first, they can hold their gangling wings up for only a moment. Soon, however, they begin to turn to face the wind and to stretch out their long, narrow wings, to let the breezes lift them a few inches into the air. Later, and for hours on end, they hold their wings out and practice running—really, just hopping, walking, and stumbling—into the wind. Unexpectedly, sometimes, the wind lifts them several feet off the ground and this seems to be so frightening that the startled birds fold their wings and legs. Of course, they fall in a tangle of awkward

White feathers begin to peep through the heavy brown down, and the chick starts to exercise its wings.

wings and legs, perhaps on top of other youngsters, who are quite naturally upset. They fight it out.

A few minutes later, as soon as everything and everyone is back in its proper place, a particularly venturesome bird may try again. This time, a gust may turn it over in the air and plop it down on its back. Then, because its outstretched wings keep it from rolling sideways to regain its feet, the young bird slowly and painfully does a comical somersault to get up. But, get up it does . . . and tries once more.

This practice in running, in flying, and in just staying upright in the nesting colony is important, for soon the father and mother will feed their offspring for the last time. The chick's days in the sandy nest on land are almost over. For most of the time in the next twenty years that the albatross may live, it will be on its true home—the rolling, blue Pacific Ocean.

5. Leaving for the Sea

In late June, when the first-hatched young Laysan Albatrosses are five months old, they leave their nests to straggle toward the ocean. By then, they look like their parents, and their bodies, bills, legs, and wings are as large. Only their black bills, dark legs and feet, and a neckstrip of ruffled feathers distinguish them.

The young trip over rocks and twigs and their own paddlelike feet. When they take to the air, they can coordinate their floppy wings barely long enough to stay aloft for fifty yards. But their maturing internal "clocks," a complicated timing system of glands and nerves, force them to leave. Besides, they are hungry.

They walk, stumble, and fly short distances, always upwind. Each one is guided by instinct, the sound of the breaking surf, and the direction of the wind. Eventually, in about three weeks, all the surviving chicks reach the beaches. Most of the parents are far at sea when their young leave. No older brothers or sisters

A young Laysan, newly arrived at the beach, gets its first view of the waters in the lagoon.

are there to guide the fledglings. These brothers and sisters of earlier years are already at sea, too. This year's crop of chicks must journey and survive by its own efforts.

The thousands of young albatrosses gather on the windy, barren beaches. They stand on the sloping shores and stare seaward. For many of them, it is their first sight of that endless horizon of water. Some retreat into the scraggly bushes behind the beach, away from the wind-driven sand and the hot summer sun. Most of the birds, however, soon make circling and short practice flights out over the greenish waters of the lagoon and return safely to the beach. Some cannot make it back to the beach and land on the water. A few of the stronger birds fly beyond the

41

Another ungainly youngster attempts to fly toward the beach.

protective reef and out of sight of the island on their very first flight.

Some fledglings resting on the water drown when waves upset them and displace their feathers. Water soaks them, and the unfortunate youngsters can no longer stay afloat. Others disappear in a flurry as a shark rises to the surface and takes an easy meal. Hordes of predatory sharks, ten to twenty feet long, gather in the lagoons of the albatross islands to feast on unwary and inexperienced young albatrosses. One blue shark we caught, on a half-inch bolt sharpened and bent into a hook and baited with half of a spoiled roast beef, had thirteen young albatrosses in its stomach.

Some of the birds try so often to leave they become exhausted and perish on the beach, which by the end of summer is littered

42

with bones and feathers. But this is according to the age old rule that only those best able to care for themselves can survive. One summer, we counted our marked fledglings on the beaches and found that nine of ten departed safely.

Those young on the open sea, and already away from the gathering of sharks, still have many things to learn. Their first ocean journey, more than two thousand miles, is to be completed in two months. The birds must toughen up flight muscles scarcely used before and learn to take advantage of the smallest currents of wind. Fortunately, the gentle summer trade winds near the breeding islands blow constantly from the east and northeast, and nudge the novices southwest when they fly and when they rest on the sea. Ocean currents also transport them west and south, toward the great, tropical Kuroshio Current.

This current then bears them northward until, to the east of

The youngsters gather on the beaches just before leaving Midway for the first time.

A more experienced and co-ordinated young albatross takes off from a sand dune near the beach.

Japan and the Kurile Islands, it hits head-on the cold Oyashio Current, roaring southward from the Bering Sea. In these tempestuous seas, most young albatrosses remain for nearly two years. It is the "nursery" for all juvenile Laysans. Here they perfect their techniques of landing and taking off from water. They become aware of noises and vibrations in the water below, possible signs of enemies.

Most importantly, they learn exactly what squid, the favored albatross food, are like. They learn how to recognize them, for these birds saw none of the squid their parents fed to them. Also, since they have always been fed squid without any effort on their part, they naturally don't know how to catch them. To learn this, they must first find where the squid are located.

44

Squid are more abundant in the cooler, richer waters where colliding currents create turbulent seas that are high in oxygen, minerals, and the microscopic plants and animals which the squid eat. The nursery is such a place. The waters around the western Aleutian Islands are also good squidding areas for older juveniles and adults.

Squid come in many sizes and shapes. Some weigh four hundred pounds and are more than thirty feet long. Albatrosses will peck away at the floating, dead carcasses of such large squid, but they prefer small, live squid, the loligos, which are six to ten inches long and weigh only a few ounces. These slender and tube-shaped animals swim backwards by jetting water from their mouths. The albatrosses catch them, probably at night, when millions of squid, packed almost solidly into great schools, rise to the surface. At least, scientists think this is how and when the albatrosses feed, but nobody has ever reported watching a Laysan Albatross catch squid. And no one knows how many squid an adult bird needs to consume each day. We albatross specialists do know that eight or ten or a dozen may make a meal for a chick, because we have counted as the adults disgorged squid to feed their nearly grown chicks in early summer.

Wind and water, and the birds' instincts, have brought them to this good feeding ground. Even so, learning to recognize and catch squid takes months of trial-and-error experiments. The young can only become skillful by practice. Perhaps that is why albatrosses have no family responsibilities until they are seven to nine years old. Before that time, learning to survive and to live like albatrosses demands all their attention.

Their first months in the nursery are difficult. New problems must be solved each day. As we have said, sharks are an ever-present danger. Nets and hooks of Japanese fishermen accidentally snare off-guard birds. Vicious typhoons swipe across the nursery, scattering the birds and drowning some. Experience is a severe teacher, but the survivors become adept at escaping from their enemies and in flying and landing and swimming. Especially important is the fact that they can now catch squid quite handily. The day will come when each bird must find enough squid for a chick and for itself.

As the Laysans learn these things, they also grow up physically. Within a year, their black bills turn horn color. Their scaly legs and feet become a soft, clean gray from being bathed in salt water. The white feathers on the body sparkle, cleansed of Midway's dirt and sand. The short feathers behind and below their eyes are pastel gray, which reduces the glare of light reflected from the water and makes it easier for the birds to see. The long, dark, tattered flight feathers of the wings and tail drop out (molt), one by one, and are replaced by new feathers. The albatrosses are gleamingly well groomed, and they always will be, for they are clean and neat birds.

The "clocks" inside their bodies, set even before the chicks broke out of their shells, are ticking away, marking the passage of time. They sound preliminary warnings of future events. One of the first messages starts some young birds flying toward Midway in May of their second year.

As usual, each bird moves at its own pace, but thousands of birds of the same age are now migrating, converging on their homes. They are fewer than when they left Midway, because only half have survived to return this first time. Even fewer will live to visit in later years. The survivors are a select group, the strongest and most skillful of the young. Among the birds flying the ocean sky are those that will produce future generations of Laysan Albatrosses on the albatross islands.

6. Lord of the Ocean Sky

While the albatross is traveling, it needs no powerful jet engine to propel it through the misty sky. As we mentioned before, the albatross uses instead the nearly constant winds and the currents of air that flow upward from the waves. When the wings are fully spread, the bird locks them into position for less tiring flight. The long pinion feathers on the ends of the wings make tiny adjustments to differences in air flow and air density, as it wheels and glides almost without effort. A seven-foot span of narrow, tapering wings and only seven streamlined pounds make an excellent gliding machine. The Laysan Albatross in flight is a beautiful example of "poetry in motion."

Flight can sometimes be difficult, however. Wind currents may blow the wrong way, into the bird's face, and then it must flap its wings. To reach a specific destination, the albatross zigzags toward it, angling across the flowing air, first in one direction and then in another, tacking like a sailboat toward its goal. When it flaps into the wind, the Laysan rockets higher but loses speed. Then it uses the gained altitude as the upper end of a swift, gliding trail down and back across the invisible, but keenly felt, helpful flow of air. Seldom more than a hundred feet above the tossing sea, it alternately flaps and glides. The glides provide brief rest periods for the large breast muscles. In this way, the albatross can cruise hundreds of miles in a single day.

Other ornithologists studying on Midway Atoll once shipped some adult Laysans in airplanes to the state of Washington and then released them. The albatrosses promptly headed for home. On their return flight, the birds traveled an average of at least three hundred miles per day, to arrive at their destination in ten days. Their top speeds probably reached fifty or sixty miles per hour.

The albatross has no equal among birds in long-distance flight over the deep salt waters of the world. It is monarch of the ocean skies.

They obviously enjoy being in the air and they fly, even when they aren't going anywhere in particular. Wind currents hit the sand and coral and low bushes on the edges of their island breeding grounds and bounce upward. Albatrosses play in these moving masses of air. They use the rising currents as phantom elevators to ascend a hundred or more feet, without a single wing beat. Then they sail along the leading edge of the rushing air in the same way that a person body-surfs on breaking waves. The albatrosses leave at the top of the elevator air shaft and fly fifty or so yards seaward, then they swoop in graceful arcs at wave height and skim along the crest of one wave before slipping over to the next wave. To board the same or another elevator, they need only turn sharply landward. As they bank to turn, one wing may cut a groove in the water's surface and act as

The Laysan Albatross is a
graceful flying machine
over the sea.

One wing tip cuts the water and serves as a brake when the albatross turns sharply to investigate an object in the ocean.

a brake to reduce slippage on the turn. This cycle of play is often repeated a dozen times.

But away from its island, the albatross—if he or she isn't migrating or catching squid—sleeps on the surface of the water. With long wings folded close to its body, and head tucked beneath the shoulder feathers, the bird is a watertight, seaworthy craft. With its dual layers of protective and buoyant feathers, the albatross floats high and dry, secure in rolling troughs between surging waves or in the spindrift atop breaking swells generated by subarctic winds.

The male is completely free on the restless sea and in the sky, when he has no egg to incubate or chick to feed. He travels and eats and sleeps when he chooses. Not even his mate, when he has one, accompanies him. She, of course, has the same freedom.

50

When an albatross takes off from a quiet sea, its feet leave little water-spout tracks.

Neither one seeks any other Laysans or ever stays long with any chance companions. Flocks of albatrosses are unusual, small in number, and temporary; birds come and go constantly. No male or female touches down on continental land. Seldom does one visit any island except the one where it was hatched.

Other albatrosses neither warn it about sharks or other enemies, nor help it to escape when in danger. The birds find their own squid, although, after a long, squidless search, an individual may join other feeding albatrosses briefly.

The albatrosses search far for food, but obtaining drinking water is no problem. It is all about them. They quench their thirst on salt water. Humans and animals die if they drink salt water. Albatrosses become paralyzed and die if they don't drink salt water. The excess salt which the albatrosses get from the salt

These fledgling albatrosses are ready to be unloaded from our barge at Lisianski Island.

water is soon distilled from their blood by a pair of slender, pink glands—one above each eye. The clear, salty waste runs to the nostrils down thin tubes (the same as the tear ducts to your nose). Then it flows into a narrow groove on each side of the bill and, finally, drips off the end of its three-and-one-half-inch length. This removal of salt is continuous, so the albatrosses must always have seawater to replenish their body salts.

Some kinds of birds flock to help each other navigate, that is, find the way to the place to which they are going. The albatross of Midway has known its home atoll's location ever since it was a nestling. It requires no assistance from other albatrosses to find that small speck of land in later years. The bird is never lost, never unaware of its destination, though storms may blow it far off course. The navigational signposts or cues of the albatross—

the sun, moon and stars, and perhaps some wind and water currents—guide it. Scientists are still trying to figure out just which of these the bird uses, and how.

We tried to find at least part of the answer in 1962, by moving banded fledglings to other islands. The youngsters were five months old. One hot July day, we gathered up two thousand of these young birds and loaded them on a steel barge, which was covered so they could not see the ocean, the sun, the moon, or the stars as we towed them to Lisianski Island, 250 miles away. We closed other young birds in cardboard boxes and flew them to Kure Island, fifty miles away.

We knew that none of these birds could see any cues, and we thought the metal of the barge and airplane would block any magnetic signals. We hoped they would learn the new cues to the island to which we had moved them. But not one has ever been found on Lisianski or Kure! Instead, seven years later, we caught the banded survivors in the fields where they were hatched on Midway. They must have learned the location of their original homes before we moved them, and remembered it for several years.

But we still hadn't found out what their signposts were or exactly when they were learned. So, we exchanged two hundred banded chicks between nests on Eastern Island and the nests on Sand Island, when they were only one month old. Even at this early age, some of them knew the strangeness of their foster nests where other chicks had started life, on an alien island, and wandered off in search of their original homes. The chicks that accepted their new parents and homes soon learned the cues to them, for they returned there to breed in later years. Another part of the answer had been found. Laysans on Midway obtained their mental image of its position in the Pacific when they were about a month old.

Eight years later, we marveled each time we found one of these banded birds on its egg on the exchange island we had chosen for it. And we still wonder what guided it to its new home, instead of to its birthplace.

Although no one knows how the Laysan Albatross finds its way over the trackless water, it is truly a bird of the open sea, a pelagic bird, as the ornithologists say. It comes to land only to find a territory, to select a mate, and later to breed. And then, it stays on land just long enough to raise a chick.

7. Strangers in Their Own Homes

Although the young birds described in Chapter 5 had conquered the seas, their homeland was now a half-forgotten memory. They had matured in the rough waters three hundred miles northeast of Japan. In the late spring of their second year, they were moving slowly southeast, toward Midway. There was no urgency in their travel and sometimes they stopped to feed for several days.

They arrived at Midway, one by one, in the middle of May. Flying a few feet above the waves, they approached the edge of the island in daylight. They rose higher in the air and cruised back and forth in the helpful currents, searching for a suitable landing strip. Finally, they alighted on the edge of the land. Getting down was painful or hilarious, depending upon whether one was an incoming albatross or a watching person. Fitful air currents and inexperience turned this first landing on solid

Some albatrosses, returning to their homes after many months at sea, belly-flop on their first landings.

ground into a comedy. Birds crashed with resounding thuds, protected from injury only by their thick down and heavy breast muscles. Arrivers bowled over Laysans already on the ground. Many, understandably, lost their tempers. Bills snapped and clattered like miniature machine guns. Occasionally, a young albatross came down awkwardly and rolled end over end among the startled nestlings. Adults on the ground snatched at the dangling toes of birds flying too low overhead.

A great many young albatrosses made a circus of their first reappearance on Midway, and this ruffled their composures, as well as their feathers.

Our particular two-year-old male skidded in, and his bill chiseled a groove in the coral rubble. The wind at his rear spread his tail feathers like a fan and raised his back feathers on end.

The bird rose quickly . . . and, just as suddenly, fell sideways, off balance. He stood up . . . and fell again. When he finally made it to his feet, he looked around, as if to see whether other albatrosses had observed the poor show. He carefully folded his wings against his body and twitched them an extra time. The feathers on the all-important, long wings had to be straight and overlapped properly. Then he flicked his bill several times, to rearrange the breast and shoulder feathers. He shook himself, to complete the job, and *moo*ed to the sky.

Since he didn't yet know quite what to do or how to behave, he stood and watched the activities silently. Minutes later, he made his way toward the home colony, a quarter-mile farther inland, tracing the route he had used to reach the beach when he left the island on his first seaward journey. The walk was torture. Sharp coral tore his water-softened webs and toes, and leg muscles, not used to supporting his weight, soon tired. He bumped into other albatrosses, who clacked their bills at him. Quite by

An old, experienced male has chased away our young male and now screams his victory.

The Sooty Tern colony erupts into a clamoring bedlam when it is disturbed by an albatross or a person.

accident and ignorance, he stepped into an adult male's territory. He had to duck his head and run to escape the irate bird. And, to make matters worse, the defending male screamed his victory cry and called the shameful retreat to the attention of all the neighbors. Even a fuzzy chick dared to snap at him.

He walked into the edge of a Sooty Tern colony, and the terns rose in a noisy, hysterical flutter of black and white bodies. They dive-bombed and blanketed him with droppings. These parents were defending their tiny gray babies, not long out of the egg, against this great, lumbering bird. He retreated and carefully walked around the rest of the densely packed terns.

The first night was just as bewildering to our young male albatross. Strange sounds pounded his ears. Nights at sea—except for stormy ones—had been quiet. There was only the soft swish of the wind and waves. But here the night air was shattered by the ghostly moans of courting shearwaters, the staccato growls of Fairy Terns, balancing on swaying branches, and the hubbub of thousands of albatrosses. Finally, he found a young albatross that tolerated him. He sat down nearby, rolled to the left to put his right foot into its feather pocket on the right side of his breast, and then rolled back to the right, to tuck in the left foot. These feathery socks kept his bare feet from chilling on the moist, cold ground. The two birds slept in fitful snatches.

The next day was no better. Out of curiosity, our young albatross approached a Red-tailed Tropic Bird, incubating an egg under some bushes. He eased his bill down toward the smaller bird, in friendly albatross fashion. The response was a raucous scream and a jab from the needle-sharp, red bill of the mother bird. He backed up in a hurry. The island was so unfriendly that, at noon, he flew to sea without having reached the place where he was hatched.

His behavior was typical of that of many of the young albatrosses, who also were rebuffed on Midway, and we shall use his experiences to represent those of all the novice Laysans.

A young bird's third-year return is very much like that of the second year, but it comes back a week or so earlier and *may* stay a day or so longer on each successive visit during the year.

In following the life cycle of our albatross, it is good to keep in mind that the age is determined by breeding season years, not calendar years. The "birthday" is when the egg was laid that produced the chick. A chick hatched on February 1, 1972, is said to be a year old on or about November 28, 1972.

In his fourth year, on April Fool's Day, our male landed at dawn on Midway, as the rising sun cast flickering shadows onto

Pairs of Fairy Terns perch in the ironwood trees above the thousands of noisy young albatrosses.

A Hawaiian Tern sits quietly on its nest in the tree above our territory-seeking young male.

The Red-tailed Tropic Bird on its egg does not tolerate even the curiosity of the male albatross.

the restless water surging and ebbing on the beach. He was better acquainted with albatross ways by now and walked rapidly inland, toward the home colony. He avoided other males and detoured around all adults feeding chicks. He circled the Sooty Tern colony, which showed that he was learning to keep out of trouble. Finally, he found an unoccupied spot next to the base of an ironwood tree and rested there. The next day, he was run off by the screaming owner of that spot, a big male who had just returned from feeding at sea. He moved to a new location. Right away, he was challenged by another, older male and forced to retreat. For two days, the young Laysan was routed from place after place by males protecting territories and shrieking defiance even after he ran away. Discouraged, he left for the hospitable sea.

Our albatross stayed four days on a more successful visit to his home colony three weeks later. The internal urge to find a place for himself on this island was growing. He came back there for five more days during the final week of May. It was his third visit this year. During the last two of these days, he rested on a bare, sandy place, only eighty feet from where he was hatched. There, his sister, this year's chick of his parents, sat in the nest, but the two never met—and they would not have known each other, anyway. However, no bird of any kind challenged his right to be there.

In early March of his fifth year, our male came back to Midway and went straight to the place where he had rested undisturbed on his previous trip. It was occupied by an older albatross, who threatened him! He halted six feet away . . . but he did not retreat as he would have when he was younger. He had some rights, although they might not be to that particular place where his enemy stood watching him. He rested on his breast, facing the older bird who finally decided to ignore him.

The following day, the much more confident young male squirmed around on the sand and, with his feet and belly, made a saucerlike bowl about twelve inches across. It was his first nest, unfinished and crude, but his. He pulled green leaves off a shrub and dropped them into the hollow. He rested in the nest for four days before leaving.

In twelve days, he returned. The hot sun had dried up his nest leaves, and the wind had filled the bowl with fine sand. He made another symbolic nest in the same spot, and watched warily each albatross that came by. Not one challenged his possession. His older challenger was nowhere in sight. Once, he stood up, bowed and whistled to a female. She came over, touched his bill with hers . . . and walked off. He raised his bill and gave a soft call, a *moo*, directed to the sky. She turned her head toward him but continued moving away. He flew off after two days.

On the return of our young albatross, ten days later, in the first week of April, he found a younger male sleeping in his bowl! He charged without warning, thrusting out his open bill and flapping his wings hard. He rolled the younger male out of the nest, and it scuttled off without a fight. Proudly erect, our male gave a victory scream, his first. It was soft and wavery. Again, he proclaimed his ownership and defiance. It was more satisfactory, although still amateurish. As his confidence increased, other Laysans recognized that his actions were no longer those of a visitor. He behaved like an owner. Territory-seeking males, young and old, did not contest his ownership. The first step toward reproducing his kind was accomplished.

After a nap in the rare warm sun of that spring day, he bowed and whistled to five females strolling nearby. Four came closer and two actually touched bills with him. The fifth female lingered to rest under a bush, three yards away. He arched his neck, bowed and whistled at her. She got up and walked over to him. They touched bills, and he, in excitement, bowed so low his bill hit the ground. Again they touched bills, and she sat down near him. After a moment's hesitation, he settled next to her and nibbled gently at the feathers on the back of her neck . . . and suddenly, with no warning, she walked away. She began to run. Spreading her wings into the wind, she sailed out of sight. It was not yet her time to pair with any male.

Our male *moo*ed to the sky once and began enticing other females. Many females his age were wandering about in the colony, but only one touched bills with him. He busied himself during the next two weeks pulling leaves into his nest and inviting females to come and get acquainted.

By now it was almost May and time for his final departure of the year. His ownership of a territory meant constant responsibilities, mainly to let every bird nearby know that this bit of land was his. Never, so long as he lived, would this spot be without some reminder of him during the albatross breeding season. If all went well in future years, his presence or that of his mate or his chick would indicate his possession.

His fifth year had been eventful. He had staked out a territory. He had defended it successfully. He had become acquainted with some females who would also return from the sea the following season. Then he could get on with the next major project —securing a mate.

8. Winning a Mate

It was a typical winter scene in the North Pacific region. The skies were lead gray and the air was near freezing. The seas surged and churned under the force of the wind until the long rollers broke into frothy whitecaps, tumbling south and east. The cold blast from the northwest blew heavy spray from the top of one breaker into the spume of the next. The traditional blue calm of the Pacific was gone, and the angry ocean made a lie of its name. Worse was to come, on this particular February day, for a midwinter storm had already lashed the Sea of Japan, scattered the fishing sampans, and shaken the buildings on the Japanese islands. Now, its fury approached the tens of thousands of Laysan Albatrosses searching for squid.

The whistling wind struck in the early darkness of night. The birds did no more than try to stay afloat, because albatrosses do not fly on dark nights. The congregations of birds in the steep-

64

sided troughs between waves were soon invisible, covered with white spray. Each bird became isolated in its own misty world, out of sight and sound of all others of its kind.

Wind and waves joined forces to carry the albatrosses southeast, nearly five hundred miles from the squidding area. But in this stormy sea, location was unimportant. Sheer survival was the thing. Catching squid was impossible. No squid ventured out of the calm dark depths into the roiling surface where an albatross could reach it with a beak. For the next five days of whipping winds and bursting seas, the birds lived on fat stored earlier in layers just beneath the skin.

The storm was difficult for birds never before so buffeted by wind and water. The weakest died. The older ones, wiser and more experienced in the ways of endurance, fared much better. As the winds slowed to breezes and the churning waves subsided into smooth rollers, the younger albatrosses went north, back to the fishing grounds. The season for *their* migratory trip to Midway was still a month or more away. But birds at least six years old were given notice from within, by those "clocks" regulated by the changing seasons, that it was time for yet another, very important journey—to find lifelong mates.

The "clocks" in the males always signalled sooner than those in the females of the same age. The males responded more quickly to the signals, and they were the first to turn homeward. This year—and forever afterward—these males would arrive on Midway a week or so ahead of their females.

The young male whose experiences we have been describing hesitated not at all when he arrived on Midway. The cues learned while he was a baby in the nest, and on earlier visits, served him well now. He flew to the center of Sand Island, turned into the wind, and glided earthward on set wings. Six feet above the ground, he let down his landing gear—his legs—

The six-year-old male wheels in for a landing and uses his webbed feet as brakes and rudders.

and spread wide the webbed toes. The webs served as air brakes to slow his flight and as rudders to balance him in the uncertain air currents. He alighted, more skillfully than in previous years, near his home colony.

A gentle breeze wafted through the cool wintry sunshine, to tease apart the feathers of the few adults. Month-old chicks, dressed in tangled gray, awoke and raised up to peer at our young albatross over the rims of their nests. He folded his wings and straightened out some misplaced feathers. After gazing at the sky for a long time, he sat resting for twenty minutes. Again, he looked skyward in all directions . . . then rose and walked awkwardly for a few feet. He angled off on a new heading and, once more, studied the sky. After still more changes in his course and fixing his eyes on the heavens many times, he halted. This was the place, his place. This was the exact spot he had claimed and defended the year before. This was *his* territory.

During the next week, the unpaired females of his age began

to arrive. They wandered and visited briefly at the invitation of different males. As an unattached female came near our male, he drew himself up to his fullest height and thrust out his snowy white breast, standing on tiptoe to be even more impressive. He eyed each female closely. He bowed and whistled and, if a female came close enough, he touched her bill, bowed low and *eh eh*ed to her. If she rested on his territory or bill-touched again, he nibbled at her neck feathers. As their mutual feeling increased, they rested side by side and nibbled and preened each other for hours on end. Sometimes, after a day or so of this close association, they began a courtship dance. More often, however, the female went on her way—to the sea or to another male.

We watched one particular flirt visit twenty-seven different males in a single day. She greeted and bill-touched and excited each one in turn before sauntering on to the next conquest. No

He raises on tiptoes and pushes out his breast whenever a female walks past.

male could follow her. Each was rooted to his home base, forced to remain there.

Territory-seeking younger males started to filter into the colony now. Each time our male returned from a trip to the sea, he was apt to find a strange male in his territory. Such intruders were no longer problems. They ran off when he came close, for he was the owner, and, in some way unknown to humans, they realized it. A month passed and, although dozens of unpaired females came to him, not one lingered on.

In the long and complicated process of Laysan mate selection, mutual attraction comes slowly, and the female makes the final choice. At this early stage, the male rejects no female. A female either stays or leaves of her own free will. If she stays long enough, courtship moves on to the next phase—the dance.

The albatross dance is a delightful ritual to watch. It is a series of postures, movements, and sounds, acted out alternately or simultaneously by the dancers. These acts are a part of albatross culture and are passed on to each succeeding generation. After the usual greeting—the touch of the bills that shows the two birds are friendly—the male begins the ceremony.

The male invites the female to dance by facing her and bowing, just as a man may do as a gracious gesture to a lady, and exhales a soft, gruntlike call, *eh eh eh eh*. He raises one partly folded wing, never both at once, and puts his bill beneath the base of the uplifted wing. The bill softly *thunk, thunk, thunks* there. Then he points it straight skyward and strains up on tiptoes. The female watches all this quietly or, sometimes, touches his expanded breast with the tip of her bill, for she is not yet ready to dance. He stares at her in rapt attention and clatters very rapidly the upper and lower halves of his bill. The *chop chop chop chop* sounds like two pieces of wood hitting together. The birds touch bills, and she reaches down to toss a twig aside. She

68

Our male strains upward and stays motionless when a female shows an interest in him . . .

. . . and clatters his bill rapidly as she faces him.

The two young birds, which become the pair whose story we tell, begin their first real courtship dance.

is stimulated and excited by the male's actions. He throws some grass, bows to the ground, and *eh eh*s again. They touch bills once more, and she touches his breast and raises one wing.

At last, she accepts his invitation to dance. Both birds tremble with excitement, and the dance tempo increases. The male quickly raises his right wing and tucks his bill beneath it. The female immediately lifts her left wing and tucks her bill beneath it. Then each lowers its wing and both point their bills straight up. Their bodies strain toward the sky, so tense that they wave slowly from side to side. They lower their heads to bill touch. He lifts his left wing while she gazes at his breast, then touches it. He stares and whinnies as she lifts her right wing. Now they gaze at one another, and each clatters its bill. The pair bob up and down rapidly, touch bills gently, and bounce on their toes.

Now, he raises his right wing, she her left. Bills go skyward,

70

As is the way of all new pairs of albatrosses, they spend hours resting together and preening each other.

and the birds become motionless statues, supported only by the very tips of their toes. After a few seconds, each bird lowers its bill and points toward the partner. Both shake their heads and bills so swiftly the action is only a blur. They bill-touch and circle and throw twigs and gravel and grass in a rite that seems symbolic of nest-building, a prophecy of things to come.

They dance all over again, doing the same things in the same way for more than an hour before they rest and gently preen each other's heads. In the soft, cool light of a full spring moon, they may dance time after time.

The friendly conclusion of a dance shows that the birds have progressed toward becoming mates. They are attracted to one another. The female has accepted the male, at least as a temporary partner. She has passed his test of her size. If her bill had reached higher than his, when both of them pointed skyward in

71

the dance, he would have attacked and driven her away. Few male albatrosses accept taller females. Both birds know instinctively by now that they can subdue their own individualities enough to dance together. Time and dancing and being together, just as with people, determine whether they will become mates.

Our pair of six-year-olds danced often during the remainder of that season and all the next season, to test the strength of this bond between them. If the pair-bond was weak, it would break and they would search out new partners. If, on the other hand, the bond between the two was fairly strong and weathered the first few tests, each successful springtime dance made it even more durable. The longer they associated, the more intimately they became acquainted. The pair-bond became increasingly firmer, and they were better prepared for reproduction. But their actual mating was still a year and a half away.

9. First Nesting

The difficult early years at sea and of visiting the colony prepare the albatrosses for the main event in their lives—reproduction, so that there will always be Laysan Albatrosses. Each trial, each experience measures their ability to escape danger, to find squid, to navigate successfully over the ocean, and to obtain a mate. Once a young male and his particular female have passed these tests, they associate as an engaged pair for nearly two years, in late winter and early spring. The behavior of each is interlocked with the behavior of the other, to form a pattern of actions suitable for raising a chick. They firm and fix memories of one another that will not be forgotten, though they may be apart for weeks or even months, as we have related.

These separations are a necessary part of the lives of albatrosses. Remember that the only islands suitable for nesting are hundreds, even thousands, of miles across the sea from the best places for squidding. The members of the pair alternate between incubation duties and feeding at sea, during the sixty-five days of incubation. One member, of course, must always be on the egg, while its mate is feeding at sea to gain weight for its next turn at incubating. During five or more months of chick feeding, the mates are on different schedules and seldom meet. When the chick is grown, the two parents go to sea, probably separately and not to be with one another until they meet on their home ground several months later.

Almost exactly six months after the last land-bound meeting of our pair in May of their seventh year, the male walked into the colony. It was dawn of the first day of December. All around him, older birds quietly incubated in their conelike nests. Some slept soundly, others only dozed, but all of them ignored him completely. His territory was vacant. He moved onto it rapidly and *mooe*d to the sky. Passing females paid no attention to his halfhearted enticing, as they hurried to their own mates and nests, tending to their own affairs. Once in a great while, a female stopped a moment and bill touched. One danced a little with him. He waited a week before going to sea for water. He stayed overnight. Two days after his return, his chosen female appeared.

She was ten yards away and half-walking, half-running toward him when he recognized her. He stared hard for a moment, bowed, and then whinnied. He trembled and bounced on his toes, and stepped toward her before his invisible ties to the territory stopped him. The nearer she came, the faster she ran, the more aroused he grew. He whinnied and whistled and bowed until she was close enough to touch bills.

They *eh eh*ed to each other, and the male tossed a few small twigs. He clattered his bill and snapped at the sky a couple of

74

The reunited pair touches bills.

times. He toe bounced and strutted around her. She sank down to rest, and he nibbled at the short gray feathers on her head. He circled her, bowed, *eh eh*ed, and preened her neck. After resting alongside her for a moment, he rose to circle again.

The years of preparation had served well, for the birds recognized each other immediately and needed no long preliminaries before they mated.

In the misty, dim light of the following morning, they flew into the northwest wind coming over the reef, en route to their first oceanic honeymoon. Where they went, we do not know. Perhaps they were together, perhaps not. But in these five days, the egg grew to weigh three-fourths of a pound, or more than a tenth of the weight of the female. As the egg's hard shell formed within her, she moved back toward Midway.

She arrived alone on the male's territory in midmorning and immediately started a nest in her chosen spot. Lying first on one side and then the other, and scratching with the three sharp claws on each foot, she hurriedly dug a slight depression the

Right after laying the egg, the female sits on the new sandy nest.

size and shape of a large dinner plate. It was none too soon, for the egg was ready to be laid.

It was one o'clock, and late in the day and season for any albatross to drop an egg. Hers was the last egg deposited in the colony that season. The experienced females and most of the young ones had laid their eggs in the mornings before mid-December. In the years to follow she, too, would lay sooner.

Right now, she was exhausted. She sank onto the egg, spread her wings slightly, and dozed. After an hour, our female rose over the egg and bent backwards to get it into the incubation pouch.

Experienced males relieve their females no later than twenty-four hours after the egg is dropped. This female's mate, our special male, was young and inexperienced, so he didn't return for a week. The female had deserted their home territory by then because her own instincts for staying on the large and hard egg were not yet well established. Strong winds had blown sand over the shallow nest. The male tried several times to get the cold and partly buried egg into his pouch. Finally, he walked away, and sat in the lee of a nearby bush for two days. The wind blew more sand, and the egg was buried forever.

The female returned early in January. The nest was completely gone, destroyed by winter storms. She stayed just one day and missed the male's next visit by a week. In late January, the two chanced to be together on the territory. They preened each other and danced briefly before departing. He returned four days later; she came in after nine days, but he was gone. They met at the territory in March, twice in April, and once in late May.

Such visits are not accidental or meaningless. They strengthen the bonds that hold the pair to their bit of land and to one another. And each time, the male's presence in a particular spot is a sign of ownership to all his neighbors.

Nor are the unsuccessful attempts at breeding wholly tragic, or unusual. Few young albatrosses are successful in their first

Their nest, abandoned and overgrown with grass, continues as their meeting place for the remainder of the year.

The young female albatross, whose story we have told, guards her very first chick.

breeding, but even these losses provide useful experience for the future. The reproductive life of albatrosses has been lengthened to make up for these early failures. The birds have a dozen or more seasons to raise chicks.

Our young pair returned to try again the very next year, when they were nine years old, and did succeed in raising a chick. In the years ahead, they will rear more chicks, to help carry on the saga of the Laysan Albatross.

Index

79